Barron's Regents Exams and Answers

Three-Year Sequence for High School Mathematics (Course I)

June 1987 Examination

Includes:

- A full-length New York State Regents Examination
- Complete answers with in-depth explanations

This Regents Supplement is supplied free of charge to insure that you get the latest exam when you buy Barron's Regents Exams and Answers.

 BARRON'S Educational Series, Inc., New York

Examination   June 1987
Three-Year Sequence for High School Mathematics — Course I

PART ONE

DIRECTIONS: *Answer 30 questions from this part. Each correct answer will receive 2 credits. No partial credit will be allowed. Write your answers in the spaces provided. Where applicable, answers may be left in terms of π or in radical form.*

1 Solve for x: $3.5x + 5.4 = 19.4$ 1 _____

2 A purse contains 3 quarters, 4 dimes, 2 nickels, and 2 pennies. If one coin is pulled out of the purse at random, what is the probability the coin will be worth exactly 10 cents?   2 _____

3 A basketball player made 9 out of 12 foul shots. What percent of his foul shots did he make?   3 _____

4 The probability that Tim will be elected president of the freshman class is 0.7. What is the probability that Tim will *not* be elected president?   4 _____

5 The length of the hypotenuse of a right triangle is 13 centimeters and the length of one of the legs is 12 centimeters. Find the number of centimeters in the length of the second leg.   5 _____

6 In the accompanying diagram, parallel lines $\overleftrightarrow{AB}$ and $\overleftrightarrow{CD}$ are cut by transversal $\overleftrightarrow{EF}$. If $m\angle 2 = 72$, what is $m\angle 1$?

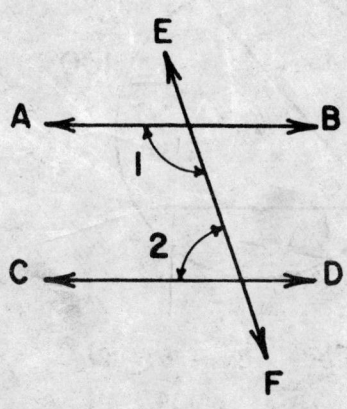

6____

7 Solve for x: $\dfrac{x}{2.5} = \dfrac{10}{25}$

7____

8 If one of the base angles of an isosceles triangle has a measure of 54, find the measure of the vertex angle.

8____

9 The mean of four numbers is 5. Find the sum of the four numbers.

9____

10 What is the value of $R^2 S$ if $R = 5$ and $S = -2$?

10____

11 Express, in terms of π, the circumference of a circle whose diameter is 14.

11____

12 In the accompanying figure, the measure of minor arc *AB* is 100. Find the measure of inscribed angle *ACB*.

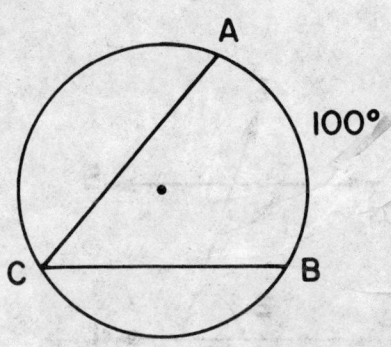

12____

13 Solve for *x* in terms of *b*: $3x - b = 2b$

13____

14 In the accompanying diagram, $\overleftrightarrow{AB}$ and $\overleftrightarrow{CD}$ intersect at *E*. Angles *AEC* and *DEB* measure $2x - 6$ and $6x - 50$, respectively. Find the value of *x*.

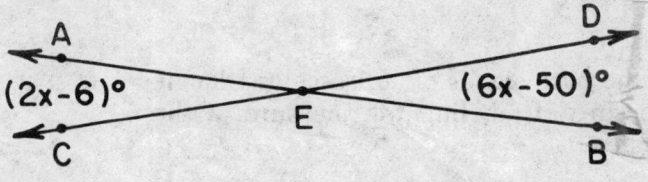

14____

15 Two complementary angles are in the ratio of 4:5. Find the measure of the *smaller* angle.

15____

16 Factor: $x^2 - 5x + 6$

16____

17 Express $\frac{x}{2} + \frac{2x}{3}$ as a single fraction in lowest terms.

17____

DIRECTIONS (18–34): *For each question chosen, write in the space provided* e numeral *preceding the word or expression that best completes the statement* answers the question.*

3 If Debbie has 3 blouses and 4 skirts, how many different outfits of a blouse and skirt can she wear?

(1) 12   (3) 3
(2) 7   (4) 4   18____

9 The solution of the equation $3(x + 3) = 12$ is

(1) 1   (3) 3
(2) 2   (4) 4   19____

0 If the length of each side of a triangle is doubled, then its perimeter

(1) remains the same   (3) is multiplied by 4
(2) is multiplied by 2   (4) is increased by 4   20____

1 Let p represent "Ann can climb Mount Everest" and let q represent "The weather is clear." Which statement represents "If the weather is clear, then Ann can climb Mount Everest"?

(1) $p \wedge q$ (3) $p \rightarrow q$
(2) $p \vee q$ (4) $q \rightarrow p$ 21____

2 If a group of data consists of the numbers 2, 2, 5, 6, and 15, which statement is true?

(1) median > mean   (3) mode < median
(2) mean = mode   (4) median = mode   22____

23 The sum of $3x^2 + x - 7$ and $x^2 + 10$ can be expressed as

(1) $4x^4 + x - 3$ (3) $3x^4 + x - 3$

(2) $3x^2 + x + 3$ (4) $4x^2 + x + 3$ 23_____

24 The product of $7y^3$ and $4y^5$ is

(1) $11y^8$ (3) $28y^8$

(2) $11y^{15}$ (4) $28y^{15}$ 24_____

25 Which inequality is the solution of $5x - 1 < 29$?

(1) $x > 7$ (3) $x < 6$

(2) $x < 7\frac{1}{4}$ (4) $x > 5\frac{3}{5}$ 25_____

26 The point $(k,3)$ lies on the graph of the line whose equation is $2x + y = 17$. What is the value of k?

(1) 7   (3) 11

(2) 10   (4) 23   26_____

27 The lengths of the sides of a triangle are 8, 15, and 17. If the longest side of a similar triangle is 51, what is the length of the *shortest* side?

(1) 32   (3) 16

(2) 24   (4) 4   27_____

28 Which statement is always true when p is false?

(1) $p \lor q$ (3) $p \land q$

(2) $p \longrightarrow q$ (4) $\sim p$ 28_____

9 What is the solution for the following system of equations?

$$2x + y = 7$$
$$x - 2y = 6$$

(1) (3,1) (3) (−1,4)
(2) (1,3) (4) (4,−1)

29____

0 The sum of $\sqrt{12}$ and $5\sqrt{3}$ is

(1) $10\sqrt{3}$ (3) $7\sqrt{3}$
(2) $7\sqrt{6}$ (4) 360

30____

1 What is the contrapositive of the statement $q \rightarrow \sim p$?

(1) $p \rightarrow q$ (3) $p \rightarrow \sim q$
(2) $\sim p \rightarrow q$ (4) $\sim q \rightarrow p$

31____

2 What is the slope of the line whose equation is $y = 2x - 10$?

(1) $\frac{1}{2}$ (3) 5

(2) 2 (4) −10

32____

3 Which expression is undefined if $x = 2$?

(1) $\frac{2}{x - 2}$ (3) $\frac{2}{x}$

(2) $\frac{x - 2}{2}$ (4) $(x - 2)(x + 2)$

33____

34 Which open sentence is represented by the graph below?

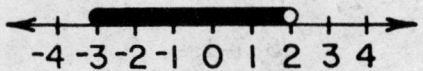

(1) $-3 < x < 2$ (3) $-3 \leq x \leq 2$
(2) $-3 \leq x < 2$ (4) $-3 < x \leq 2$ 34___

DIRECTIONS (35): *Leave all construction lines in the answer.*

35 Using compass and straightedge, construct a triangle congruent to triangle ABC. Use $\overline{A'B'}$ as one side of the congruent triangle.

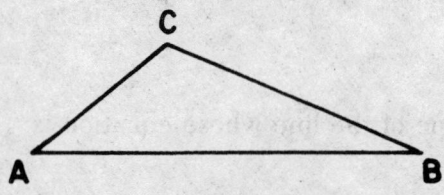

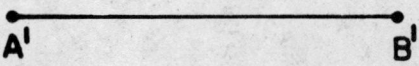

35___

PART TWO

DIRECTIONS: *Answer four questions from this part. Show all work unless otherwise directed.*

36 *a* On the same set of coordinate axes, graph the following system of inequalities:

$$y < -2x + 3$$
$$y - 3x \geq -2 \quad [8]$$

b Write the coordinates of a point in the solution set of the inequalities graphed in part *a*. [2]

37 Solve algebraically and check:

$$4x + 3y = 12$$
$$-2x + y = -16 \quad [8,2]$$

38 In the accompanying figure, $\triangle ABC$ is inscribed in circle O, $\overline{AC}$ is a diameter of circle O, $AC = 8$, and $\overset{\frown}{AB} \cong \overset{\frown}{BC}$.

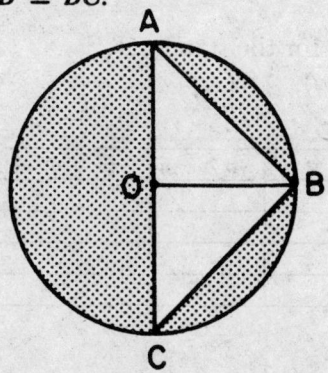

a Find the measure of minor arc *AB*. [2]
b Find the measure of $\angle BOC$. [2]
c Find the measure of $\angle ABC$. [2]
d Find the area of $\triangle ABC$. [2]
e Find the area of the shaded region. [Answer may be left in terms of π.] [2]

39 The sum of the measures of three angles is 200. These measures are in the ratio 3:5:12. Find the measures of the three angles. [*Only an algebraic solution will be accepted.*] [5,5]

40 One positive number is one more than another positive number. The sum of the squares of the two numbers is 85. Find both positive numbers. [*Only an algebraic solution will be accepted.*] [5,5]

41 Eight of Mrs. Smith's students weigh 79, 60, 80, 50, 55, 100, 80, and 72 pounds. If one of the students is picked at random, find the probability that the student's weight will be:

a greater than the mean [4]
b exactly equal to the median [4]
c less than the mode [2]

42 Complete the truth table for the statement
$\sim (p \vee q) \leftrightarrow (\sim p \wedge \sim q)$. [10]

	1	2	3	4	5	6	7
p	q	$\sim p$	$\sim q$	$p \vee q$	$\sim (p \vee q)$	$\sim p \wedge \sim q$	$\sim (p \vee q) \leftrightarrow (\sim p \wedge \sim q)$
T							
T							
F							
F							

Answers June 1987

Three-Year Sequence for High School Mathematics—Course I

ANSWER KEY
PART ONE

1.	4	13.	b	25.	(3)
2.	$\dfrac{4}{11}$	14.	11	26.	(1)
		15.	40	27.	(2)
3.	75	16.	$(x - 3)(x - 2)$	28.	(4)
4.	0.3	17.	$\dfrac{7x}{6}$	29.	(4)
5.	5			30.	(3)
6.	108	18.	(1)	31.	(3)
7.	1	19.	(1)	32.	(2)
8.	72	20.	(2)	33.	(1)
9.	20	21.	(4)	34.	(2)
10.	-50	22.	(3)	35.	construction
11.	14π	23.	(4)		
12.	50	24.	(3)		

Part Two—*See* Answers Explained.

ANSWERS EXPLAINED
PART ONE

1. The given equation contains decimals:

$$3.5x + 5.4 = 19.4$$

Clear decimals by multiplying all terms on both sides of the equation by 10:

$$10(3.5x) + 10(5.4) = 10(19.4)$$
$$35x + 54 = 194$$

Add -54 (the additive inverse of 54) to both sides of the equation:

$$\underline{\ -54 = -54}$$
$$35x = 140$$

Divide both sides of the equation by 35:

$$\frac{35x}{35} = \frac{140}{35}$$
$$x = 4$$

$x = 4$.

2. Probability of an event occurring equals

$$\frac{\text{number of favorable cases}}{\text{total possible number of cases}}$$

Since there are 4 dimes in the purse, the number of favorable cases for pulling out at random one coin worth 10 cents is 4.

The 3 quarters, 4 dimes, 2 nickels, and 2 pennies constitute a total of 11 coins. Therefore, the total possible number of cases for pulling out one coin is 11.

The probability of pulling out one coin worth 10 cents is $\frac{4}{11}$.

The probability is $\frac{4}{11}$.

3. Percent of shots made equals $\dfrac{\text{number of shots made}}{\text{total number of foul shots taken}}$

The percent of foul shots made if 9 were made out of 12 shots taken equals

$$\frac{9}{12} = \frac{3}{4} = 75\%$$

The percent is **75.**

4. Let x = the probability that Tim will *not* be elected.

It is certain that Tim will either be elected or not be elected. Certainty is represented by a probability of 1. It is given that the probability that Tim will be elected is 0.7:

$$x + 0.7 = 1$$

Add -0.7 (the additive inverse of 0.7) to both sides of the equation:

$$\underline{-0.7 = -0.7}$$
$$x \qquad = \quad 0.3$$

The probability that Tim will *not* be elected is **0.3.**

ALTERNATIVE SOLUTION: Probability equals

$$\frac{\text{number of favorable cases}}{\text{total possible number of cases}}$$

If the probability that Tim will be elected is 0.7 or $\dfrac{7}{10}$, then he must receive 7 votes out of every 10 votes cast. Thus, for every 10 votes cast, there will be 3 votes that are not for him. For the probability of *not* being elected, the 3 votes not for Tim represent the number of "favorable" cases, and the 10 votes cast represent the total possible number of cases. Therefore, the probability of Tim's *not* being elected is $\dfrac{3}{10}$ or **0.3**.

5. Let x = the number of centimeters in the length of the second leg.

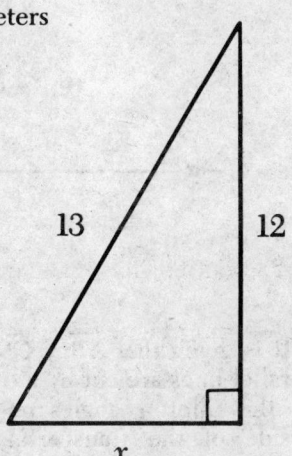

By the Pythagorean Theorem, in a right triangle the sum of the squares of the lengths of the legs equals the square of the length of the hypotenuse:

$$x^2 + 12^2 = 13^2$$

Square 12 and square 13, and insert these values into the equation:

$$x^2 + 144 = 169$$

Add -144 (the additive inverse of 144) to both sides of the equation:

$$\begin{aligned} -144 &= -144 \\ \hline x^2 &= 25 \end{aligned}$$

Take the square root of each side of the equation:

$$x = \pm\sqrt{25} = \pm 5$$

Reject the negative root as meaningless for a length:

$$x = 5$$

The second leg is **5** cm long.

ALTERNATIVE SOLUTION: 5-12-13 is one of the "Pythagorean triples." Since the largest number, 13, is the hypotenuse as required for the use of this shortcut, the remaining leg must be **5**.

6.

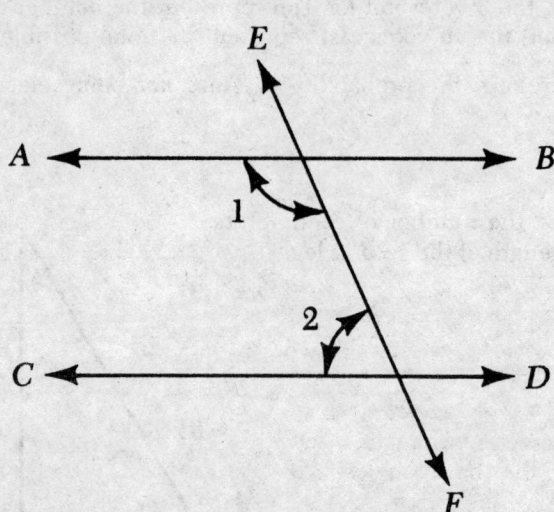

It is given that $\overleftrightarrow{AB} \parallel \overleftrightarrow{CD}$. If two parallel lines are cut by a transversal, the interior angles on the same side of the transversal are supplementary:

$$m \angle 1 + m \angle 2 = 180$$

It is given that $m \angle 2 = 72$:

$$m \angle 1 + 72 = 180$$

Add -72 (the additive inverse of 72) to both sides of the equation:

$$\frac{-72 = -72}{m \angle 1 \quad = 108}$$

$m \angle 1 = \mathbf{108}$.

7. The given equation has the form of a proportion (two equal ratios):

$$\frac{x}{2.5} = \frac{10}{25}$$

In a proportion, the product of the means equals the product of the extremes (cross-multiply):

$$25x = 10(2.5)$$
$$25x = 25$$

Divide both sides of the equation by 25:

$$\frac{25x}{25} = \frac{25}{25}$$
$$x = 1$$

$x = \mathbf{1}$.

8.

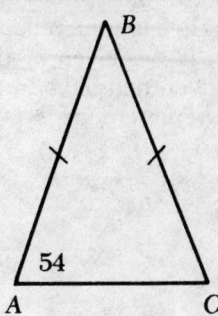

The sum of the measures of the three angles of a triangle is 180:

$$m \angle A + m \angle B + m \angle C = 180$$

In an isosceles triangle, the measures of the base angles are equal: $m \angle A = m \angle C = 54$:

$$54 + m \angle B + 54 = 180$$

Combine like terms:

$$m \angle B + 108 = 180$$

Add -108 (the additive inverse of 108) to both sides of the equation:

$$\frac{-108 = -108}{m \angle \qquad B = 72}$$

The measure of the vertex angle is **72**.

9.   Let x = the sum of the four numbers.

The mean of several numbers is obtained by dividing their sum by the number of them. Therefore, if the mean of the four numbers is 5:

$$5 = \frac{x}{4}$$

Multiply both sides of the equation by 4 to clear fractions:

$$4(5) = 4\left(\frac{x}{4}\right)$$

$$20 = x$$

The sum of the four numbers is **20**.

10.   The given expression is:

$$R^2S$$

Since $R = 5$ and $S = -2$, substitute these values for R and S in the given expression:

$$(5)^2(-2)$$

First square 5:

$$25(-2)$$

Then perform the indicated multiplication:

$$-50$$

The value is **-50**.

11.   The circumference, C, of a circle whose diameter is d is given by the formula:

$$C = \pi d$$

It is given that $d = 14$:

$$C = \pi(14) = 14\pi$$

The circumference is **14π**.

12.

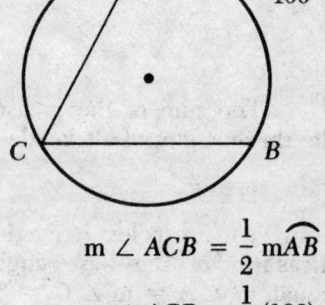

The measure of an inscribed angle is equal to one-half the measure of its intercepted arc:

$$m \angle ACB = \frac{1}{2}\ m\widehat{AB}$$

$m\widehat{AB} = 100$:

$$m \angle ACB = \frac{1}{2}(100)$$

$$m \angle ACB = 50$$

The measure of $\angle ACB$ is **50**.

13.   The given equation is a *literal* equation: $3x - b = 2b$

To isolate the term containing x on one side, add b (the additive inverse of $-b$) to both sides of the equation:

$$\begin{array}{r} b = b \\ \hline 3x = 3b \end{array}$$

Divide both sides of the equation by 3:

$$\frac{3x}{3} = \frac{3b}{3}$$

$$x = b$$

$x = b$.

14.

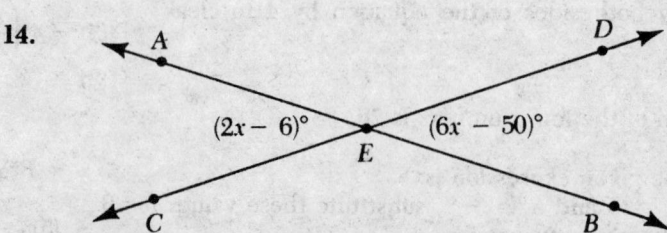

$\angle AEC$ and $\angle DEB$ are *vertical angles*.

Vertical angles are equal in measure: $m \angle AEC = m \angle DEB$

Substitute the given values: $2x - 6 = 6x - 50$

Add $-2x$ (the additive inverse of $2x$) and also add $+50$ (the additive inverse of -50) to both sides of the equation:

$$-2x + 50 = -2x + 50$$
$$44 = 4x$$

Divide both sides of the equation by 4:

$$\frac{44}{4} = \frac{4x}{4}$$
$$11 = x$$

$x = 11$.

15. Let $4x =$ the measure of the *smaller* angle.

Then $5x =$ the measure of the *larger* angle since the angles are in the ratio $4 : 5$.

If two angles are complementary, the sum of their measures is 90:

$$4x + 5x = 90$$

Combine like terms:

$$9x = 90$$

Divide both sides of the equation by 9:

$$\frac{9x}{9} = \frac{90}{9}$$
$$x = 10$$
$$4x = 4(10) = 40$$

The measure of the *smaller* angle is **40**.

16. The given expression is a *quadratic trinomial*:

$$x^2 - 5x + 6$$

A quadratic trinomial can be factored into the product of two binomials. The factors of the first term, x^2, are x and x, and they become the first terms of the binomials:

$$(x \quad)(x \quad)$$

The factors of the last term, $+6$, become the second terms of the binomials, but they must be chosen in such a way that the product of the inner terms added to the product of the outer terms equals the middle term, $-5x$, of the original trinomial. Try -3 and -2 as the factors of $+6$:

$$-3x = \text{inner product}$$
$$(x - 3)(x - 2)$$

Since $(-3x) + (-2x) = -5x$, these are the correct factors:

$$-2x = \text{outer product}$$
$$(x - 3)(x - 2)$$

The factored form is $(x - 3)(x - 2)$.

17. The fractions in the given expression have different denominators:

$$\frac{x}{2} + \frac{2x}{3}$$

The least common denominator (L.C.D.), that is, the smallest number into which each of the denominators will divide evenly, for 2 and 3 is 6. Convert each fraction to an equivalent fraction having the L.C.D. by multiplying the first fraction by 1 in the form $\frac{3}{3}$, and the second fraction by 1 in the form $\frac{2}{2}$:

$$\frac{3x}{3(2)} + \frac{2(2x)}{2(3)}$$
$$\frac{3x}{6} + \frac{4x}{6}$$

Fractions having the same denominator may be combined by combining their numerators over the common denominator:

$$\frac{3x + 4x}{6}$$

Combine like terms:

$$\frac{7x}{6}$$

The single fraction in lowest terms is $\frac{7x}{6}$.

18. Each of Debbie's 3 blouses may be matched with each of her skirts to make a different outfit. Therefore, the number of different outfits is 3×4 or 12.
The correct choice is **(1)**.

19. The given equation contains parentheses:
$$3(x + 3) = 12$$
Remove the parentheses by applying the distributive law to multiply each term within the parentheses by 3:
$$3x + 9 = 12$$
Add -9 (the additive inverse of 9) to both sides of the equation:
$$\frac{-9 = -9}{3x \quad = \quad 3}$$
Divide both sides of the equation by 3:
$$\frac{3x}{3} = \frac{3}{3}$$
$$x = 1$$

The correct choice is **(1)**.

20.

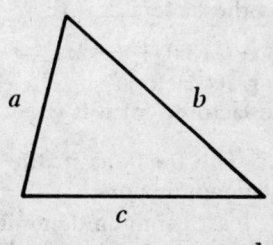

The perimeter, P, is the sum of the lengths of the three sides of the triangle:

$$P = a + b + c$$

If each side is doubled, the new perimeter, P', is given by:

$$P' = 2a + 2b + 2c$$

The right side contains a common factor of 2:

$$P' = 2(a + b + c)$$

Since $P = a + b + c$:

$$P' = 2P$$

The new perimeter equals the old perimeter multiplied by 2.

The correct choice is (2).

21. Given: p = Ann can climb Mount Everest, and q = the weather is clear.

"If the weather is clear, then Ann can climb Mount Everest" is the *implication* (also called the *conditional*), $q \rightarrow p$.

The correct choice is (4).

22. The given data are: 2, 2, 5, 6, 15

The *mean* equals

$$\frac{\text{sum of the items}}{\text{number of items}} = \frac{2 + 2 + 5 + 6 + 15}{5} = \frac{30}{5} = 6$$

The *median* is the middle item when the items are arranged in order of size; the median in this case is 5.

The *mode* is the item occurring most frequently; the mode in this case is 2.

Examine each choice in turn:

(1) median $\overset{?}{>}$ mean: $5 \not> 6$ false
(2) mean $\overset{?}{=}$ mode: $6 \neq 2$ false
(3) mode $\overset{?}{<}$ median: $2 < 5$ true
(4) median $\overset{?}{=}$ mode: $5 \neq 2$ false

The correct choice is (3).

23. To add polynomials, write one under the other with like terms in the same column:

$$\begin{array}{r} 3x^2 + x - 7 \\ x^2 \qquad + 10 \\ \hline 4x^2 + x + 3 \end{array}$$

Add each column algebraically:

The correct choice is (4).

24. The product of the monomials is represented by:

$$(7y^3)(4y^5)$$

To multiply two monomials, first multiply their numerical coefficients to obtain the numerical coefficient of the product:

$$(7)(4) = 28$$

Multiply the literal factors to obtain the literal factor of the product, remembering that powers of the same base are multiplied by adding their exponents:

$$(y^3)(y^5) = y^8$$

Put the two results together:

$$(7y^3)(4y^5) = 28y^8$$

The correct choice is (**3**).

25. The given inequality is:

$$5x - 1 < 29$$

Add $+1$ (the additive inverse of -1) to both sides of the inequality:

$$\frac{+1 = +1}{5x \qquad < 30}$$

Divide both sides of the inequality by 5:

$$\frac{5x}{5} < \frac{30}{5}$$

$$x < 6$$

The correct choice is (**3**).

26. If a point lies on the graph of an equation, the coordinates of the point must satisfy the equation. Since $(k, 3)$ lies on the graph of $2x + y = 17$, substitute k for x and 3 for y in the equation:

$$2k + 3 = 17$$

Add -3 (the additive inverse of 3) to both sides of the equation:

$$\frac{-3 = -3}{2k \qquad = 14}$$

Divide both sides of the equation by 2:

$$\frac{2k}{2} = \frac{14}{2}$$

$$k = 7$$

The correct choice is (**1**).

27. Let $x =$ the length of the *shortest* side of the similar triangle.

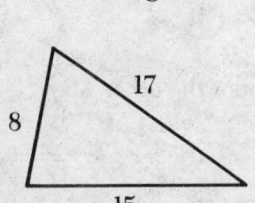

In similar triangles, corresponding sides are in proportion. Here the shortest side of the similar triangle, length x, will correspond to the shortest side, 8, of the first triangle, and the longest side, 51, will correspond to the longest side, 17, of the first triangle:

$$\frac{x}{8} = \frac{51}{17}$$

Reduce the fraction on the right by dividing numerator and denominator by 17:

$$\frac{x}{8} = \frac{3}{1}$$

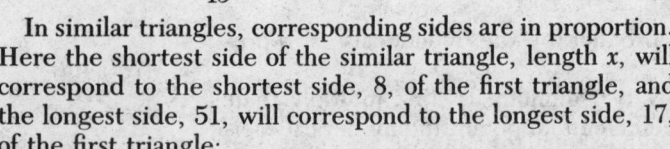

In a proportion, the product of the means equals the product of the extremes (cross-multiply):

$$x = 3(8)$$
$$x = 24$$

The correct choice is (2).

28.   Consider each choice in turn:

(1) $p \lor q$ is the *disjunction* of p and q. The disjunction is true if either p or q or both are true. Thus, it is not always true when p is false; it will not be true if p and q are both false.

(2) $p \leftrightarrow q$ is an *equivalence relation*, or *biconditional*, between p and . The biconditional is true if p and q have the same truth value, that , if both are true or both are false. It is false if their values are different. Thus, $p \leftrightarrow q$ will be false if p is false and q is true.

(3) $p \land q$ is the *conjunction* of p and q. It is true when both p and q are true, and false if either of them or both are false. Thus, it is never true when p is false.

(4) $\sim p$ is the *negation* of p. Its truth value is opposite to that of p. Thus, when p is false, $\sim p$ is always true.

The correct choice is (4).

29.   The given system of equations is:

$$\begin{cases} 2x + y = 7 \\ x - 2y = 6 \end{cases}$$

Multiply each term of the first equation by 2:

$$4x + 2y = 14$$

Add the original second equation to eliminate y:

$$\underline{x - 2y = 6}$$
$$5x = 20$$

Divide both sides of the equation by 5:

$$\frac{5x}{5} = \frac{20}{5}$$
$$x = 4$$

Substitute 4 for x in the original first equation:

$$2(4) + y = 7$$
$$8 + y = 7$$

Add -8 (the additive inverse of 8) to both sides of the equation:

$$\underline{-8 = -8}$$
$$y = -1$$

The solution to the system of equations is $(4, -1)$.
The correct choice is (4).

ALTERNATIVE SOLUTION: Each choice may be tested by substituting the x and y values in *both* of the *original* equations. The correct solution must satisfy both original equations. This method will require eight test substitutions, but only choice (4) will be found to satisfy the two original equations.

30.　The radicals to be added are *not* like radicals:　　$\sqrt{12} + 5\sqrt{}$
Simplify the radicand 12 by factoring out the highest
factor that is a perfect square:　　$\sqrt{4(3)} + 5\sqrt{}$
Remove the perfect square factor from under the rad-
ical sign by taking its square root and writing it as a
coefficient of the radical:　　$2\sqrt{3} + 5\sqrt{}$
The radicals are now like radicals since they have the
same index (2 understood—for square root) and the
same radicand, 3. Like radicals may be combined by
combining their numerical coefficients:　　$7\sqrt{3}$
The correct choice is **(3)**.

31.　The given statement is the *implication*, or *conditional*:　　$q \rightarrow \sim p$
The *contrapositive* of a statement is formed by negating
the hypothesis and conclusion of the original statement and
then interchanging them. The hypothesis (or "given") of the
original statement is q, and its negation is $\sim q$. The conclusion (or "to prove") of the original statement is $\sim p$, and its
negation is $\sim(\sim p)$ or p. Therefore, the contrapositive is:　　$p \rightarrow \sim q$
The correct choice is **(3)**.

32.　If the equation of a line is in the form $y = mx + b$, then m is
its slope and b is its y-intercept. The given equation, $y = 2x - 10$, is
in the form $y = mx + b$, with $m = 2$ and $b = -10$. Therefore, it
slope is 2.
The correct choice is **(2)**.

33.　An expression is undefined if its denominator is 0, since division
by 0 is undefined. If $x = 2$:
Choice (1), $\dfrac{2}{x - 2}$, becomes $\dfrac{2}{2 - 2}$ or $\dfrac{2}{0}$.
Choice (2), $\dfrac{x - 2}{2}$, becomes $\dfrac{2 - 2}{2}$ or $\dfrac{0}{2}$ or 0.
Choice (3), $\dfrac{2}{x}$, becomes $\dfrac{2}{2}$ or 1.
Choice (4), $(x - 2)(x + 2)$, becomes $(2 - 2)(2 + 2)$ or $(0)(4)$ or 0.
Only choice (1) is undefined.
The correct choice is **(1)**.

34. The shaded line extends from -3 to 2. It includes -3, but does ot include 2 since the open, unshaded circle at 2 indicates that 2 is ot part of the set.

Thus, the graph represents the set of all numbers greater than or qual to -3, and less than but not including 2. This is the open sentence $-3 \leq x < 2$.'

The correct choice is **(2)**.

35.

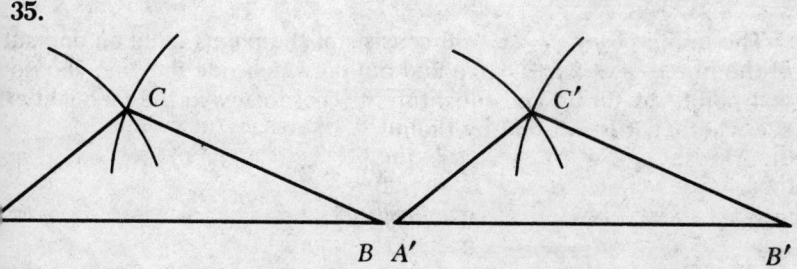

STEP 1: With A as center, open the compasses so that they span the ngth of $\overline{AC}$.

STEP 2: With A' as center and the compasses open to the length etermined in Step 1, draw an arc.

STEP 3: With B as center, open the compasses so that they span the ngth of $\overline{BC}$.

STEP 4: With B' as center and the compasses open to the length etermined in Step 3, draw an arc intersecting the arc of Step 2 in oint C'.

STEP 5: Draw $\overline{A'C'}$ and $\overline{B'C'}$.

Triangle $\underline{A'B'C'}$ is the required triangle congruent to triangle ABC d having $\overline{A'B'}$ as one side.

PART TWO

36. a. STEP 1: To draw the graph of the inequality $y < -2x +$ first draw the graph of the equation $y = -2x + 3$. Choose any three nvenient values for x, and substitute them in the equation to find the rresponding values of y:

x	$-2x + 3$		$= y$
-2	$-2(-2) + 3 = 4 + 3$	$=$	7
0	$-2(0) + 3 = 0 + 3$	$=$	3
3	$-2(3) + 3 = -6 + 3$	$=$	-3

Then plot the points $(-2, 7)$, $(0, 3)$, and $(3, -3)$, and draw a *broke* line through them. The broken line is the graph of $y = -2x + 3$; it *i* broken to indicate that the points on it are *not* part of the graph c $y < -2x + 3$.

The graph of $y < -2x + 3$ consists of the points lying on one sid of the line $y = -2x + 3$. To find out on which side they lie, choose test point, say $(0, 0)$, and substitute its coordinates in the inequality t see whether it is satisfied by them:

$$0 \stackrel{?}{<} -2(0) + 3$$
$$0 \stackrel{?}{<} 0 + 3$$
$$0 < 3 \checkmark$$

The point $(0, 0)$ satisfies the inequality, so the points on its side of th broken line represent the graph of $y < -2x + 3$. Shade this regio with cross-hatching extending down and to the left.

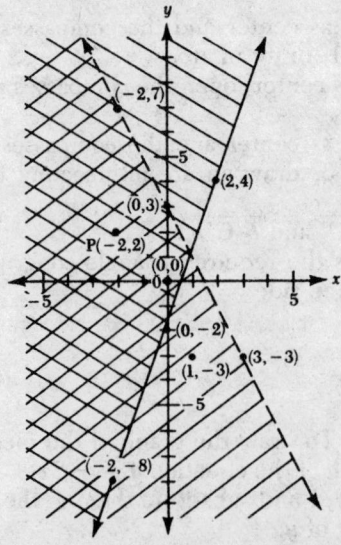

STEP 2: To draw the graph of $y - 3x \geq -2$, it is convenient to rearrange this inequality into a form in which it is solved for y.

$$y - 3x \geq -2$$

Add $3x$ (the additive inverse of $-3x$) to both sides of the inequality:

$$\frac{3x = \qquad 3x}{y \qquad \geq -2 + 3x}$$

First draw the graph of $y = -2 + 3x$ by choosing any three convenient values of x and substituting them in the equation to obtain the corresponding values of y:

x	$-2 + 3x$	$= y$
-2	$-2 + 3(-2) = -2 - 6$	$= -8$
0	$-2 + 3(0) = -2 + 0$	$= -2$
2	$-2 + 3(2) = -2 + 6$	$= 4$

Then plot the points $(-2, -8)$, $(0, -2)$, and $(2, 4)$, and draw a *solid* line through them. This line is the graph of $y = -2 + 3x$; it is solid to indicate that it is part of the graph of $y \geq -2 + 3x$. The part of the graph that represents the inequality $y > -2 + 3x$ consists of the points that lie on one side of the line $y = -2 + 3x$. To find out on which side, choose a test point, say $(1, -3)$, and substitute its coordinates to find out whether it satisfies the inequality:

$$-3 \overset{?}{>} -2 + 3(1)$$
$$-3 \overset{?}{>} -2 + 3$$
$$-3 \not> 1$$

Since $(1, -3)$ does *not* satisfy the inequality, the points on the *opposite* side of the line $y = -2 + 3x$ from $(1, -3)$ represent the graph of $y > -2 + 3x$. Shade this region with cross-hatching extending up and to the left.

b. The solution set of the system consists of all points in the region covered by *both* types of cross-hatching or by points on that part of the solid line that forms a boundary of the double-cross-hatched region. One point in the solution set is $P(-2, 2)$.

37. The given system of equations is:

$$\begin{cases} 4x + 3y = 12 \\ -2x + y = -16 \end{cases}$$

Multiply each term of the second equation by 2:

$$-4x + 2y = -32$$

Add the original first equation to eliminate x:

$$4x + 3y = 12$$

$$5y = -20$$

Divide both sides of the equation by 5:

$$\frac{5y}{5} = \frac{-20}{5}$$

$$y = -4$$

Substitute -4 for y in the original second equation:

$$-2x - 4 = -16$$

Add $+4$ (the additive inverse of -4) to both sides of the equation:

$$+4 = +4$$

$$-2x = -12$$

Divide both sides of the equation by -2:

$$\frac{-2x}{-2} = \frac{-12}{-2}$$

$$x = 6$$

The solution set is $(6, -4)$ or $x = 6$, $y = -4$.

CHECK: Substitute 6 for x and -4 for y in *both original* equations. The solution must satisfy *both*:

$4x + 3y = 12$	$-2x + y = -16$
$4(6) + 3(-4) \stackrel{?}{=} 12$	$-2(6) + (-4) \stackrel{?}{=} -16$
$24 - 12 \stackrel{?}{=} 12$	$-12 - 4 \stackrel{?}{=} -16$
$12 = 12 \;\checkmark$	$-16 = -16 \;\checkmark$

38.   a.   Since $\overline{AC}$ is a diameter, $\overparen{ABC}$ is a semicircle and $m\overparen{ABC} = 180$.

Since $\overparen{AB} \cong \overparen{BC}$, $m\overparen{AB} = m\overparen{BC}$. Thus, $m\overparen{AB} = 90$.

$m\overparen{AB} = 90$.

b. $\angle BOC$ is a *central angle*. The measure of a central angle is equal to the measure of its intercepted arc:

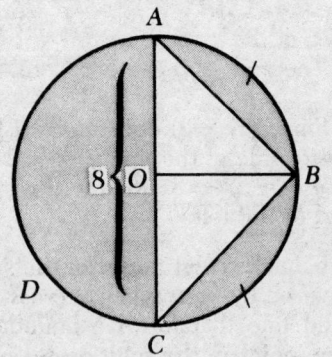

From part a, $m\overparen{BC} = m\overparen{AB} = 90$:

$$m \angle BOC = m\overparen{BC}$$

$$m \angle BOC = 90$$

$m \angle BOC = 90$.

c. $\angle ABC$ is an *inscribed angle*. The measure of an inscribed angle is equal to one-half the measure of its intercepted arc:

$$m \angle ABC = \frac{1}{2} m\overset{\frown}{ADC}$$

Since $\overline{AC}$ is a diameter, $\overset{\frown}{ADC}$ is a semicircle and $m\overset{\frown}{ADC} = 180$:

$$m \angle ABC = \frac{1}{2} (180)$$
$$m \angle ABC = 90$$

$m \angle ABC = \mathbf{90}$.

d. $AC = 8$. Since $\overline{AC}$ is a diameter, every radius of the circle has a length equal to $\frac{1}{2}$ (8) or 4. $\overline{OB}$ is a radius; therefore $OB = 4$.

$\overline{OB}$ is perpendicular to $\overline{AC}$, and therefore $\overline{OB}$ is the altitude to the base $\overline{AC}$ of $\triangle ABC$.

The area of $\triangle ABC = \frac{1}{2} AC \times OB = \frac{1}{2} (8)(4) = \frac{1}{2} (32) = 16$.

The area of $\triangle ABC = \mathbf{16}$.

e. The area, A, of a circle is given by the formula $A = \pi r^2$, where r is the length of the radius. From part *d*, $r = 4$. Therefore, the area of circle $O = \pi(4)^2 = 16\pi$.

The area of the shaded region equals the area of the circle minus the area of $\triangle ABC$. From part d, the area of $\triangle ABC = 16$. Therefore, the area of the shaded region $= 16\pi - 16$.

The area of the shaded region $= \mathbf{16\pi - 16}$.

39. Let $3x =$ the measure of the first angle.
    Then $5x =$ the measure of the second angle.
    And $12x =$ the measure of the third angle.

The sum of the measures of the three angles is 200:

$$3x + 5x + 12x = 200$$

Combine like terms:

$$20x = 200$$

Divide both sides of the equation by 20:

$$\frac{20x}{20} = \frac{200}{20}$$
$$x = 10$$
$$3x = 30$$
$$5x = 50$$
$$12x = 120$$

The measures of the angles are **30, 50,** and **120**, respectively.

40. Let x = the smaller positive number.
Then $x + 1$ = the larger positive number.

The sum of the squares of the two numbers is 85:

$$x^2 + (x + 1)^2 = 85$$

Square $(x + 1)$:

$$\begin{array}{r} x + 1 \\ x + 1 \\ \hline x^2 + x \\ x + 1 \\ \hline x^2 + 2x + 1 \end{array}$$

$$x^2 + x^2 + 2x + 1 = 85$$

Combine like terms:

$$2x^2 + 2x + 1 = 85$$

This is a *quadratic equation*. Rearrange it so that all terms are on one side equal to 0 by adding -85 (the additive inverse of 85) to both sides:

$$\frac{-85 = -85}{2x^2 + 2x - 84 = 0}$$

To simplify, divide each term on both sides of the equation by 2:

$$x^2 + x - 42 = 0$$

The left side is a *quadratic trinomial*, which can be factored into the product of two binomials. The factors of the first term, x^2, are x and x, and they become the first terms of the binomials:

$$(x \quad)(x \quad) = 0$$

The factors of the last term, -42, become the second terms of the binomials, but they must be chosen in such a way that the product of the inner terms added to the product of the outer terms equals the middle term, $+x$, of the original trinomial. Try $+7$ and -6 as the factors of -42:

$$+7x = \text{inner product}$$
$$(x + 7)(x - 6) = 0$$
$$-6x = \text{outer product}$$

Since $(+7x) + (-6x) = +x$, these are the correct factors:

$$(x + 7)(x - 6) = 0$$

If the product of two factors is 0, either factor may equal 0:

$$x + 7 = 0 \quad \text{OR} \quad x - 6 = 0$$

Add the appropriate additive inverses, -7 for the left equation and $+6$ for the right equation:

$$\frac{-7 = -7}{x \quad = -7} \qquad \frac{+6 = +6}{x \quad = 6}$$

Reject the negative value since the question calls for positive numbers:

$$x = 6$$
$$x + 1 = 7$$

The positive numbers are **6** and **7**.

41.   The eight given weights are: 79, 60, 80, 50, 55, 100, 80, 72
Rearrange these data in order
of magnitude: 50, 55, 60, 72, 79, 80, 80, 100

The *mean* = $\dfrac{\text{sum of all the weights}}{8}$ = $\dfrac{576}{8}$ = 72.

The *median* equals the middle item when the data are arranged in order of magnitude. Since there are eight items, there are two middle items: 72 and 79. In such a case, the median is defined as the value midway between them, that is, their average. The median = $\dfrac{72 + 79}{2}$ = $\dfrac{151}{2}$ = $75\dfrac{1}{2}$.

The *mode* is the item that occurs most frequently. Here the mode is 80, since 80 occurs twice and each other weight occurs only once.
Probability of an event occurring equals

$$\frac{\text{number of favorable cases}}{\text{total possible number of cases}}$$

a.   Four of the weights (79, 80, 80, and 100) are greater than the mean, 72. Thus there are 4 favorable cases out of a total of 8 possible cases for a student's weight to be greater than the mean.
The probability that a student's weight will be greater than the mean = $\dfrac{4}{8}$.

b.   Since none of the individual weights is exactly equal to the median, $75\dfrac{1}{2}$, there are 0 favorable cases for a student's weight to be exactly equal to the median.
The probability that a student's weight will exactly equal the median = $\dfrac{0}{8}$ = **0**.

c.   Five of the weights (50, 55, 60, 72, and 79) are less than the mode, 80. Thus there are 5 favorable cases out of the total of 8 possible cases for a student's weight to be less than the mode.
The probability that a student's weight will be less than the mode = $\dfrac{5}{8}$.

42.

p	q	$\sim p$	$\sim q$	$p \vee q$	$\sim(p \vee q)$	$\sim p \wedge \sim q$	$\sim(p \vee q) \leftrightarrow (\sim p \wedge \sim q)$
T	T	F	F	T	F	F	T
T	F	F	T	T	F	F	T
F	T	T	F	T	F	F	T
F	F	T	T	F	T	T	T

The column for q is filled in with truth values, T or F, in such a way that all possible combinations of values for p and q will be included.

$\sim p$ is the *negation* of p, and $\sim q$ is the *negation* of q. The truth values for these columns are the opposites of the values on the same lines in the columns for p and q, respectively.

$p \vee q$ is the *disjunction* of p and q. The truth value of the disjunction is T when either p or q or both are T, but is F when p and q are both F.

$\sim(p \vee q)$ is the *negation* of $p \vee q$. The truth values in the column for $\sim(p \vee q)$ are the opposites of those in the column for $p \vee q$.

$\sim p \wedge \sim q$ is the *conjunction* of $\sim p$ and $\sim q$. The conjunction has the truth value T when both $\sim p$ and $\sim q$ are T. It has the truth value F when either $\sim p$ or $\sim q$ or both are F.

$\sim(p \vee q) \leftrightarrow (\sim p \wedge \sim q)$ is the *equivalence relation*, or *biconditional*, between $\sim(p \vee q)$ and $(\sim p \wedge \sim q)$. The equivalence relation has the truth value T when the truth values of $\sim(p \vee q)$ and $(\sim p \wedge \sim q)$ are the same, that is, when both are T or both are F. The equivalence relation has the truth value F when $\sim(p \vee q)$ and $(\sim p \wedge \sim q)$ have different truth values.

Topic	Question Numbers	Number of Points	Your Points	Your Percentage
1. Numbers (rat'l, irrat'l); Percent	3	2		
2. Properties of No. Systems	33	2		
3. Operations on Rat'l Nos. and Monomials	17, 24	2 + 2 = 4		
4. Operations on Multinomials	23	2		
5. Square root; Operations involving Radicals	30	2		
6. Evaluating Formulas and Expressions	10	2		
7. Linear Equations (simple cases incl. parentheses)	19	2		
8. Linear Equations containing Decimals or Fractions	1, 7	2 + 2 = 4		
9. Graphs of Linear Functions (slope)	26, 32	2 + 2 = 4		
10. Inequalities	25, 34	2 + 2 = 4		
11. Systems of Eqs. & Inequal. (alg. & graphic solutions)	29, 36a, b, 37	2 + 8 + 2 + 10 = 22		
12. Factoring	16	2		
13. Quadratic Equations	40	10		
14. Verbal Problems	39	10		
15. Variation	—	0		
16. Literal Eqs.; Expressing Relations Algebraically	13	2		
17. Factorial n	—	0		
18. Areas, Perims., Circums., Vols. of Common Figures	11, 20, 38d, e	2 + 2 + 2 + 2 = 8		
19. Geometry ($\cong$, $\angle$ meas., $\parallel$ lines, compls., suppls., const.)	6, 8, 12, 14, 15, 35, 38a, b, c	2 + 2 + 2 + 2 + 2 + 2 + 2 + 2 + 2 = 18		
20. Ratio & Proportion (incl. similar triangles)	27	2		
21. Pythagorean Theorem	5	2		
22. Logic (symbolic rep., logical forms, truth tables)	21, 28, 31, 42	2 + 2 + 2 + 10 = 16		

23. Probability (incl. tree diagrams & sample spaces)	2, 4, 41a, b, c	2 + 2 + 4 + 4 + 2 = 14		
24. Combinatorics (arrangements, permutations)	18	2		
25. Statistics (central tend., freq. dist., histograms)	9, 22	2 + 2 = 4		